W9-DFE-060

THE DUST BOWL

by
John Farris

Illustrations by Maurie Manning
and
Michael Spackman
Robert Caldwell
Randol Eagles

LUCENT
B·O·O·K·S

WORLD DISASTERS

No part of this book may be reproduced or used in any other form or by any other means, electrical, mechanical or otherwise, including, but not limited to photocopy, recording or any information storage and retrieval system, without written permission from the publisher.

Look for these and other exciting
World Disasters books:

Pompeii
The Black Death
The Titanic
The Chicago Fire
The San Francisco Earthquake
The Crash of '29
The Armenian Earthquake

Library of Congress Cataloging-in-Publication Data
Farris, John, 1940-
    The dust bowl / by John Farris; illustrations by Maurie Manning.
       p.   cm. -- (World disasters)
    Bibliography: p.
    Includes index.
    Summary: Discusses the disastrous drought in the United States during the 1930s which made a 'dust bowl' out of a part of the Great Plains, causing great hardship to farmers.
    ISBN 1-56006-005-0
    1. Southwestern States--History--Juvenile literature. 2. Great Plains--History--Juvenile literature. 3. Droughts--Southwestern States--History--20th century--Juvenile literature. 4. Droughts--Great Plains--History--20th century--Juvenile literature. 5. Depressions--1929--Southwestern States--Juvenile literature. 6. Depressions--1929--Great Plains--Juvenile literature. 7. Agriculture--Southwestern States--History--20th century--Juvenile literature. 8. Agriculture--Great Plains--History--20th century--Juvenile literature. 1. Droughts--Great Plains--History. 2. Agriculture--Great Plains--History. 3. Dust storms--Great Plains. 4. Great Plains--History. I. Manning, Maurie, 1960--ill. II. Title III. Series.
F786.F32 1989   89-33557
978--dc20   CIP
                                                                 AC

© Copyright 1989 Lucent Books, Inc.
Lucent Books, Inc., P.O. Box 289011, San Diego, California, 92128-9011

This book is for Lena

Table of Contents

Preface
The World Disasters Series

World disasters have always aroused human curiosity. Whenever news of tragedy spreads, we want to learn more about it. We wonder how and why the disaster happened, how people reacted, and whether we might have acted differently. To be sure, disaster evokes a wide range of responses—fear, sorrow, despair, generosity, even hope. Yet from every great disaster, one remarkable truth always seems to emerge: in spite of death, pain, and destruction, the human spirit triumphs.

History is full of great disasters, which arise from a variety of causes. Earthquakes, floods, volcanic eruptions, and other natural events often produce widespread destruction. Just as often, however, people accidentally bring suffering and distress on themselves and other human beings. And many disasters have sinister causes, like human greed, envy, or prejudice.

The disasters included in this series have been chosen not only for their dramatic qualities, but also for their educational value. The reader will learn about the causes and effects of the greatest disasters in history. Technical concepts and interesting anecdotes are explained and illustrated in inset boxes.

But disasters should not be viewed in isolation. To enrich the reader's understanding, these books present historical information about the time period, and interesting facts about the culture in which each disaster occurred. Finally, they teach valuable lessons about human nature. More acts of bravery, cowardice, intelligence, and foolishness are compressed into the few days of a disaster than most people experience in a lifetime.

Dramatic illustrations and evocative narrative lure the reader to distant cities and times gone by. Readers witness the awesome power of an exploding volcano, the magnitude of a violent earthquake, and the hopelessness of passengers on a mighty ship passing to its watery grave. By reliving the events, the reader will see how disaster affects the lives of real people and will gain a deeper understanding of their sorrow, their pain, their courage, and their hope.

Introduction
A Decade of Drought

Beginning in 1931, a historic **drought**, or prolonged period of dry weather, descended upon an agricultural region in the central United States known as the Great Plains. Rivers shrank away from their banks, and creeks turned to sand. Livestock suffered. Fields of wheat and corn were destroyed. Only the wild grasses successfully withstood the relentless waves of heat, and even these were scorched the color of dirt. At first farmers were concerned, but not particularly discouraged. Droughts are a normal occurrence on the Great Plains, with one appearing every twenty years or so. Plains farmers were persevering and optimistic by nature. They were willing to wait for the rain.

As the drought continued into the next year, a few small windstorms, or **sand blows**, swept across the plains, scattering loose topsoil into the air. Still, farmers were not alarmed. Wind is an ever-present element on the plains. But as the decade progressed and the drought persisted, the winds blew harder, lifting dirt from the plowed fields and darkening the sky. These mile-high dust storms were called **black blizzards**, and they were terrifying to behold.

From 1931 through 1941, the unrelenting drought and its accompanying dust storms ravaged the Great Plains. After May 1934, the worst of it was centered in the five states that make up the southern plains, an area that became known as the Dust Bowl. Included were the western portions of Kansas and Oklahoma, the eastern fringes of Colorado and New Mexico, and the **panhandle** of northwest Texas.

Once a vast farmland of cultivated fields and fat cattle, the southern plains became a barren landscape of drifting sand dunes, withering crops, and dying livestock.

The Dust Bowl's Place in History

Louisiana Purchase—1803
Lewis and Clark Expedition—1804-1806

Cyrus McCormick invents reaping machine—1834

Texas admitted to U.S. as 28th state—1844
California Gold Rush—1848

Kansas admitted to U.S. as 34th state—1861
American Civil War—1861-1865
Homestead Act offers 160 acres of free land—1862

Joseph Farwell Glidden invents barbed wire—1873
Colorado admitted to U.S. as 38th state—1876

Indians of Oklahoma forced onto reservations—1889

Oklahoma admitted to U.S. as 46th state—1907
Enlarged Homestead Act offers 320 free acres —1909
New Mexico admitted to U.S. as 47th state—1912
World War I—1914-1918

Stock market crash leads to world depression—1929

Worst years of Dust Bowl drought— 1934-1935
Franklin D. Roosevelt is president of U.S.—1933-1945
World War II—1939-1945

Oklahoma declared disaster area due to drought—1954

Martin Luther King Jr. assassinated—1968
Richard Nixon resigns as U.S. president—1974

Drought in Ethiopia kills one million—1982-1984

One
The Southern Plains

Route 56 slices across the south-western corner of Kansas into Oklahoma's panhandle. In the 1930s, it was a two-lane blacktop that seemed to go on forever in a thin line that stretched out over the broad, flat plain. On this part of the southern plains, there were no trees to slow the fierce northerly winds that followed the scorching drought, and the powdery soil blew freely. After a severe dust storm, hills of sand hid all but the tops of fence posts along the roadside. Between the fence posts, clusters of tumbleweeds clung like withered fruit to the uppermost strand of barbed wire. They were a startling contrast to the huge, colorful billboards that advertised Burma-Shave or described the plush comfort of traveling by train.

Cars traveling on Route 56 shuddered as they crossed rippled dunes of sand that spilled out onto the highway. Every so often, motorists passed an abandoned farmhouse with drifts of windblown dirt piled up to the window sills, or a half-buried tractor anchored to its plow. The buildings, the machinery, the stilt-legged wooden windmills, these

hings told the travelers this was farm-
and. Yet for miles, they saw nothing
growing that was green, very few animals in the pastures, and even fewer people. The vacant landscape had the look
of a desert—dry, lifeless, and forbidding.

One Sunday morning in mid-April

1935, motorists visiting the southern
plains found the weather unseasonably
warm for springtime. Two weeks had
passed since the last dust storm, and the
windmills atop their wooden towers were
stilled. By noon, the brassy April sun was
sending wavy lines of heat rising from
the asphalt. Whenever the people in their
cars opened a window, the air rushing
in was hot and dry, gritty with dust
swirling up from the highway. It stung
their eyes until they had to squint, and it
burned their lungs when they breathed.

When the black line of highway ran
alongside the railroad tracks, visiting
motorists saw the peaked tower of a
grain elevator looming in the distance.
As late as 1931, local harvests had been
so plentiful that the elevators were filled
to capacity, and excess wheat had lain
rotting alongside them. Grain from the
southern plains had been shipped by rail
and boat to countries all over the world.
But now the massive, rusted warehouses
were empty, as were the boxcars that
sat on the tracks, their gaping doorways
inviting the dust.

Shortly after noon on this particular
Sunday, visitors and residents on the
sunny southern plains witnessed a dramatic change in the weather. The still air
grew suddenly colder, and soon the sky
was full of chattering birds. Descending
out of the north, they alighted on the
sloping rooftops and fluttered about
anxiously in the dusty yards. People felt
a sense of approaching doom. As they
looked to the north, the boiling black
cloud rolling toward them seemed a
mile high. The date was April 14, 1935.
It would be remembered by many as
the day of the worst dust storm they
had ever seen.

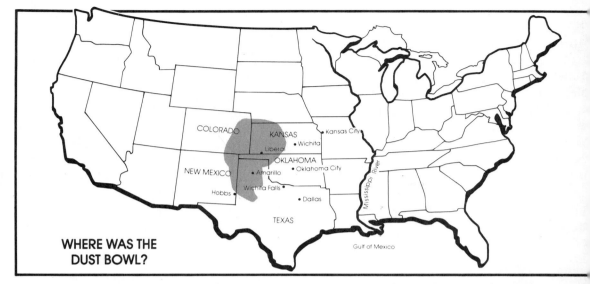

WHERE WAS THE DUST BOWL?

Dust storms occurred throughout the thirties, and as the drought continued, visitors to the southern plains were awed by the devastated landscape. Although the boundaries were shifting and imprecise, the Dust Bowl centered around the Oklahoma panhandle and the southwestern corner of Kansas. Residents of small rural towns there spent most of the decade battling sand blows, eating dust, and digging in against the awesome, destructive force of the dreaded black blizzards.

Most visitors carefully avoided the southern plains during the thirties. They feared they might be trapped in a blinding dust storm or bogged down on the dust-covered roads. But the fearsome black blizzards prompted an invasion of journalists who came to write about the ongoing disaster for their eastern newspapers. Few reporters stuck around long enough to personally witness one of the monstrous dust storms. But before they cabled in their stories and departed for home, the majority of them had recorded their observations about rural life on the southern plains. It was a far different life from what they were used to in the large cities of the East.

Their first impression was of the level, seemingly endless landscape. Except for the stony hill country in Oklahoma's extreme northwestern corner, most of the region was as flat as the desktops in a big city newsroom. Entering a rural community, an Easterner could not help but notice the lack of tall buildings. The largest structures visible on the broad plains horizon were the grain elevators, but they were small compared to buildings in cities like Chicago, New York, or Pittsburgh.

Like the elevators, most of the small town buildings were box-shaped and plain. The rooftops of most houses were steeply pitched to shed the snow or rain dropped by violent winter blizzards and sudden summer storms. The typical small town had a paved main street, with a bank, post office, general store, and cafe. Hotels were few and far between, and the visiting journalist lucky enough to reserve a room soon discovered that indoor toilets were a luxury, even in town.

Some of the more sophisticated small towns might feature a drug store and a movie theater. Most drug stores contained a soda fountain and a long counter lined with swivel chairs. The theater's tiny marquee displayed the name of the movie currently playing, often with a missing letter or two.

Unlike eastern cities, the southern plains offered little or no night life, since most of the local residents were home and in bed by ten o'clock. A few towns, however, had a pool hall where farmers and their hired hands sometimes gathered in the evenings for a game of eight ball or dominoes. Inside, farmers debated familiar topics: Who would win the National League pennant? Would President Franklin Roosevelt's new administration help strengthen the economy?

Inevitably, though, the talk would turn to the crops and the unpredictable weather. Despite the dust storms and the wheat crops withering in the fields, farmers played down their hardships and spoke hopefully of the future. During the course of an evening, more than one farmer would wistfully declare that "one good rain'll make a fortune for us all."

Southern plains farmers were not only persevering and optimistic, they were also just plain stubborn. They had to be in order to survive the disastrous decade of the 1930s. Many were the grandchildren of rugged pioneer settlers who had built their first houses out of **sod** during the homestead era a half-century earlier. Farming on the southern plains was usually a family enterprise, and it was not uncommon to find three generations—grandparents, parents, and children—working side by side. The men usually worked in the fields and the women in the kitchens, although a plainswoman's chores often took her outside the home as well.

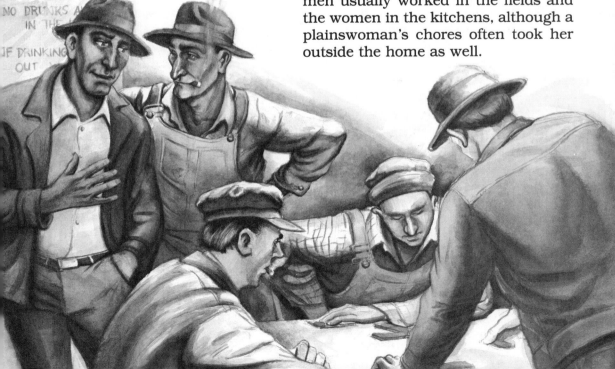

Southern plains farmers began their day at first light and ended it at sundown, and they spent most of it in backbreaking labor. Fields needed plowing year-round. Crops had to be planted on schedule and harvested as soon as they ripened. The farmer either developed the necessary grit, strength, and stamina, or found another line of work. Those who put off their chores for another day usually paid for it in lost profits.

Although the gasoline-powered tractor had been in common use for more than a decade, not everyone could afford one. Many farmers still cultivated their fields using the old wooden-handled plows. They bent down the brims of their hats to shield their eyes from the sun and walked behind a team of plodding horses or mules. By midmorning their hands were blistered from gripping the high curving handles, and their faded denim overalls were drenched with sweat.

Farmers who could afford tractors and other new labor-saving machines worked long, hard days, too, but they accomplished more with less effort. Using the new machines, a wealthy farmer or a hired hand could do more in a single day than two people using *draft* animals could do in two weeks. Whether farmers plowed using tractors or mules, they were ready for a hearty supper and a good night's sleep when the day's work was done.

A typical farm family lived in a one-story wood-framed house, usually in need of paint. Rooms inside these houses were small and drab. A worn sofa and a rickety dinner table with wooden chairs furnished the living room. Cheap, floral-print wallpaper was sometimes added for a dash of color. Bedrooms contained little more than beds and a few pegs on the walls for hanging clothes. In the kitchen, open shelves served in place of cupboards, and the cooking was done on a wood-burning stove that also provided heat for the house in winter. During warm weather, a kerosene-burning stove that put out less heat replaced the wood-burner.

The farmer's wife ran the household and worked equally as hard as her husband. Rising with him at dawn, she cooked his breakfast, and while he was *tilling* the fields, she was milking cows and tending the family vegetable garden. Using a variety of folk remedies, she treated her family's injuries and did her best to cure their ailments. She also supervised the chores of the older children, who were expected to feed the hogs, chickens, goats, and cows, as well as help their mother with the milking.

Not only was the kitchen a place for cooking, it also served as the work center of the home. A plainswoman did all of her laundry, ironing, sewing, and canning in the kitchen. On laundry day, she soaped and scrubbed the clothes in a tub, using a **washboard**, then she dropped them in a kettle of boiling water to rinse. Only a few of the farmhouses had electricity or refrigeration. Most women ironed clothes with a **flatiron** heated on the stove, and they did their sewing on a pedal-operated sewing machine.

Since there was no indoor plumbing in most of these homes, the family used an outhouse and bathed in a tub in the kitchen, drawing buckets of water from a nearby well.

During the months of late summer and fall, women preserved ripe fruit and garden vegetables in air-tight **Mason jars**. Corn was combined with bell peppers, lima beans, and spices to make a mouth-watering succotash. The women stewed tomatoes and pickled cucumbers to be served as side dishes, and the preserved peaches, apples, and cherries were used in cobblers and pies. They stored the jars of food in a storm cellar under the house. This way a family enjoyed their favorite garden delicacies throughout the year.

Of course, some farmers lived better than others. Families owning farms of several thousand acres had earned huge profits during the bountiful wheat harvests of the 1920s. These well-to-do farmers dressed fashionably and drove shiny new cars. They bought the latest farm tools and machinery and hired local farm hands or **migrant workers** to help with the chores. Even their barns were impressive structures, freshly painted and as solidly built as if they had been intended for human residents.

The wealthy farmers often lived in two- or three-story homes, with a bright coat of whitewash contrasting sharply with the flowered hedge and drooping elm trees. The interiors of these modest prairie mansions often contained expensive household furnishings shipped from department stores in Kansas City and Chicago. A radio encased in a gleaming

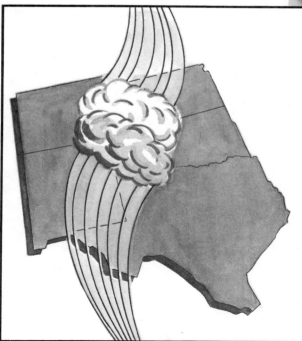

PLAINS WEATHER: CLIMATE OF EXTREMES

The sky above the southern plains is a battleground of conflicting winds. Southern plains weather is influenced both by warm, tropical air masses from the south and cold, polar air masses from the north. Most of the area's rainfall comes from moist tropical air masses moving northward from the Gulf of Mexico. Upon reaching the plains, these air masses regularly encounter the dry, heavier, polar air masses blowing southward from northern Canada.

This heavy, cool air stays close to the ground, forcing the warm, moist air to move upward. As it rises, the moist air cools, and the moisture *condenses*, or turns to rain or snow. Some of the tropical air masses collide so forcefully with the cool northern air that violent rain and thunderstorms occur.

More often, however, the warm air masses are already dry by the time they reach the southern plains. That is why this region normally receives less than 10 inches (25 centimeters) of rainfall per year.

mahogany cabinet might have occupied a prominent position in the living room, providing the entire family with news, music, comedy, and drama.

Families in such households enjoyed most modern conveniences of the day, including telephone service, indoor plumbing, and electricity. The housewives could depend on a vacuum cleaner, washing machine, and refrigerator to reduce their workload. But more often than not, they hired one of the **share-croppers'** wives as a maid.

Sometimes, owners of large farms rented out fields to farmers who could not afford their own land. These **tenant farmers** were also called sharecroppers because they gave the landowner a share of the harvest as payment for rent. Many of the sharecroppers had left failing cotton farms in the South with the hope of bettering their fortunes growing wheat on the plains. They rarely had enough money to buy their own farms, and they were grateful for a place to live and fields to cultivate, with the rent payment delayed until harvest time.

Realizing that their share of the profits depended on a successful harvest, most sharecroppers worked the rented land as if it were their own. Often they had to live in run-down, one-room shacks with dirt floors and leaky, tar-paper roofs. Older children slept two and three to a bed, and the younger ones slept with their parents. When wheat prices were up and the harvest was good, some of the sharecroppers farmed successfully and improved their standard of living. Those who farmed unsuccessfully lived difficult lives filled with despair.

Most farmers lived and worked on their farms year-round. They spent long days plowing and planting their fields. Many grew a variety of crops, raised a few cattle, and produced eggs and dairy products. But since new labor-saving machines had been introduced, people from other professions could become part-time farmers. Already assured of a steady income, many bankers, merchants, and schoolteachers living in town could afford to buy land in another part of the county and farm part-time. Sometimes they bought land in a neighboring county, or even in another state.

They were called suitcase farmers because they took a few weeks off each spring and fall to plant and harvest their crops, then returned to their regular jobs. Ample rainfall during the growing season could produce a **bumper** wheat crop even when the fields were left untended. If this happened while wheat prices were high, these suitcase farmers made enormous profits for very little work. When wheat prices were low, or when the crops failed due to dry weather or neglect, the suitcase farmers could depend upon a steady income from their regular jobs.

Plains weather helps form the region's tough but fertile soil. Rainfall, temperature, and humidity all influence the chemical content of a soil. For example, heavy rainfall causes *leaching*, which drains nitrogen and other fertile chemicals out of the soil. The brown- and chestnut-colored soils of the southern plains, however, are subject to only light rainfall, and are unleached. They are still rich in the chemical nutrients necessary for plant growth.

Over thousands of years, the other active force in forming the plains soil has been the wild grasses. Although the region's dry climate discouraged the growth of trees, the hardiness of wild grasses allowed them to flourish on the plains.

Most wild grasses are *perennials*, or plants that continue living for years. As they grow, these wild grasses create a thick sod with an expanding mass of stems and roots entwined in the soil. With their network of roots, wild grasses are well equipped to withstand drought. They absorb plenty of water and nutrients from the soil. The sod also helps hold the soil together so it does not wash away in the rain or blow away in the wind.

Weather has always been an unpredictable element of farming the *semi-arid* southern plains. The climate of an *arid* region is consistently dry, and that of a *humid* region is consistently wet. But the southern plains climate is

WILD GRASSES HELD THE PLAINS SOIL TOGETHER

Wild grasses are **perennials**, but wheat, corn, and other grains are **annuals**. Annuals die after a single growing season, but perennials continue to grow year after year. The perennial wild grasses of the southern plains produce a heavy tangle of stems and roots to form a thick carpet of *sod*. The tangle of roots hold moisture, so wild grasses withstand drought well. Also, the thick sod prevents water and wind from *eroding* the soil.

Unlike the wild grasses, grains such as wheat and corn are poorly equipped to withstand drought. Since they last only one growing season, they produce only a shallow, temporary network of stems and roots. Almost every year in the past century, farmers have planted more grains. Wherever wild grasses have been replaced by fields of wheat and corn, there is no sod to hold the soil in place. And once the grain has been harvested, the loose soil is easily eroded by wind and rain.

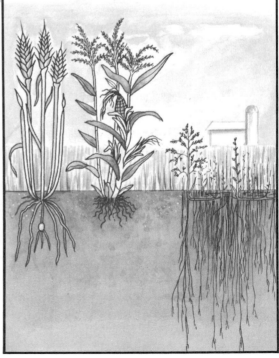

sometimes arid, sometimes humid, and sometimes in between. At times a whole year will pass without even enough rainfall to moisten the ground. Scorching winds seem sent from hell.

But late summer and autumn can also produce sudden, frightening rainstorms, frequently accompanied by hailstones the size of eggs. Crackling streaks of lightning electrify the air and roll balls of fire across the prairie. In the winter, destructive blizzards with seventy mile-per-hour (110 kilometer-per-hour) winds whip through fields and towns.

The unpredictable weather made farming on the southern plains a gamble. With the right amount of rainfall, the rich plains soil would produce abundant crops of wheat and corn. On the other hand, a prolonged drought or a sudden hailstorm could erase a year's work.

Two
Farming the Southern Plains

Just over a century ago, before ranchers and farmers settled on the southern plains, this region was a flat, sprawling wilderness covered with a remarkable variety of wild grasses. Some grew in bunches and rose taller than a man. When the prairie winds were blowing, the grass bent and rippled like waves rolling toward a beach.

The immense, rolling grassland was teeming with wildlife. Prairie dogs curiously poked their tawny squirrel-faces from the entrances of their underground burrows. Jackrabbits bounded through the tall grass in twenty-foot leaps. Fat prairie chickens nested in the sand hills formed by windblown soil, or *loess*, grown over with grass. Keeping a wary lookout for predators, herds of pronghorn antelope drank from the sandy shores of shallow, meandering rivers.

The wild, grass-covered prairie was also well populated with wolves and coyotes, rattlesnakes, high-soaring eagles and hawks, bobcats, weasels, and badgers. But of all the plains wildlife, the most majestic, the most magnificent, was the buffalo. Enormous herds of buffalo once roamed the North American grasslands. Migrating across the prairie, the herds sought out areas where the grass was most abundant. They never grazed too long in one area. As soon as the grass was too low to nibble easily, the buffalo moved on.

Whenever the buffalo moved, the Indians who lived on the southern plains followed them. The plains Indians, the earliest human inhabitants of the prairie, lived a fierce, primitive existence. Although they hunted most of the grassland wildlife, their existence revolved around the buffalo. The massive animal's meat was their main source of food. Buffalo hide and bones provided them with everything from clothing and shelter to tools and toys.

The Indians thought the buffalo would last forever. But in 1871 the era of hide hunters began. These hunters supplied the growing demands for furs in Europe and the eastern United States. An expert hide hunter could kill 200 buffalo a day. One hunter claimed to have downed 120 head in only forty minutes. It is estimated that 30 million

buffalo were killed during this period, solely for their hides. The prairie was left littered with their whitened bones.

When they realized that their way of life was about to vanish with the slaughtered herds, plains Indians resisted. Raiding parties attacked small settlements or isolated travelers. But blue-uniformed troops of the U.S. Cavalry quickly crushed the rebellion, and by 1900 most Indian tribes had been forced onto reservations.

Hostile Indians and the harsh plains weather discouraged widespread settlement of the southern plains well into the nineteenth century. Shortly before the Civil War, though, the U.S. government began encouraging people to settle there. The Homestead Act of 1862 enabled a U.S. citizen twenty-one years of age or older to file a claim for 160 acres, or a quarter-section, of public land.

The first to take advantage of this free land were ranchers. By then, the Indians were no longer a threat, and the buffalo were nearly gone, so ranchers began settling vast stretches of prairie. These early ranchers raised so many cattle on their lands that the cattle overgrazed, eating the grass so far down to the ground it took the grass a long time to grow back.

Because of the spectacular profits to be made from raising cattle, ranchers wanted the grasslands solely for their herds. They encouraged the slaughter of buffalo and pronghorn antelope that were competing with cattle for the grass. To safeguard the range for their cattle, ranchers first eliminated the larger predators such as grizzlies and wolves. When they suspected that coyotes, badgers, and eagles were menacing their livestock, they tried to eliminate them, too.

But the ranchers did not understand that the plains predators had helped to keep down the number of grasshoppers, mice, jackrabbits, and prairie dogs. Once their natural enemies were eliminated, these smaller **herbivores**, or plant eaters, multiplied in such great numbers that they, too, began to compete with cattle for the grass.

Immediately following the spring of 1886, a second wave of land-hungry settlers arrived on the plains. Farmers abandoned their soil-poor farms in the East and set out by the thousands for the prairie grasslands. These lands had been abandoned by cattle ranchers, who had lost 85 percent of their herds during the severe winter of 1885. The rangeland they left vacant was eagerly claimed by the new settlers. In a single season, hazardous plains weather had ended the cattlemen's era, and by 1890, farmers had gained control of the grasslands.

The first thing farmers needed was a reliable water supply for their crops and livestock. Not everyone could settle near a river, and during summer the small creeks often became dry, sandy ditches. Early settlers solved this problem by digging wells. Once a well was dug, water could be brought up by lowering and raising a bucket on a rope. This laborious and time-consuming task was soon eliminated by the prairie windmill.

HALLIDAY'S WINDMILL

Since their invention by the Persians in the seventh century, windmills have been helping farmers draw water from their wells. The wheel at the top of the windmill is turned by the wind. The motion of the wheel moves a *crankshaft* up and down. The crankshaft drives a pump, which pumps water up from the well.

The kind of windmill seen on most American farms has a small wheel that automatically turns sideways to the wind when the wind blows too hard. This durable windmill, often called Halliday's windmill after its inventor, Daniel Halliday, was perfected in 1854. It played an important role in helping farmers settle the arid southern plains.

turned the soil. The plow had to cut deep to break the sod matted with the roots of wild herbs and grasses. The sod was so tough that early homesteaders had cut it into bricks and used it to build their homes.

A harvesting machine popular with plains farmers during the homestead period was the **Marsh Harvester**, a platform on wheels pulled by a team of two horses. Usually, several men worked together to operate the harvester. The driver controlled the horses from his elevated seat under an awning, while two men rode alongside on the platform, or **binding deck**. As the wheat was cut, a moving canvas lifted it to the binding deck, where it was tied into **sheaves**, or bundles, by the two men.

During the homesteading period, **threshing**, or the separation of harvested grain from its straw and seed covering, did not begin until all the grain had been harvested. The old threshing machine required a crew of twenty people and several horses to operate. Usually, the owner and operator brought his machine to a particular district, where neighboring farmers served as the crew. They worked from dawn till dark, moving from farm to farm until all the harvested wheat was threshed.

Reports of bountiful harvests and available land found their way east, and a last frontier land rush occurred after Congress passed the Enlarged Homestead Act of 1909. Instead of 160 acres, each settler could now claim 320, and once again farmers set out for the plains by the thousands to stake their claims. In the three year period between 1912 and 1915, over 100,000 new homestead claims were filed.

With the addition of the windmill, farmers could finally water their livestock adequately and **irrigate** their fields during dry weather. Farms expanded, and the plains sod crumbled under the plow as fields of wheat and corn advanced into the shrinking grasslands.

Farming the plains began with busting sod, breaking the tough upper crust of soil. Before the days of mechanized farm equipment, most homesteaders used a **moldboard plow** for this job. The plow featured a curved iron plate above the cutting edge that lifted and

By 1915, a revolutionary new machine had appeared on the plains. The new machine was quick and efficient. It could be operated by a single person and seemed indestructible. This new machine was the gasoline-powered tractor.

Not everyone was an admirer of the new machine. John Steinbeck won a Pulitzer Prize in 1940 for his novel *The Grapes of Wrath*, an account of the Dust Bowl and its survivors. In it, he describes the tractor as something alive, a monster:

The tractors came over the roads and into the fields, great crawlers moving like insects, having the incredible strength of insects. They crawled over the ground, laying the track and rolling on it and picking it up. Diesel tractors, puttering while they stood idle; they thundered when they moved, and then settled down to a droning roar. Snub-nosed monsters, raising the dust and sticking their snouts into it, straight down the country, across the country, through fences, ... in and out of gullies in straight lines. They did not run on the ground, but on their own roadbeds. They ignored hills and gulches, watercourses, fences, houses.

Most farmers on the southern plains welcomed the tractor, however, particularly those who practiced summer **fallowing**. Because there was rarely enough rainfall to bring the soil back to life, plains farmers commonly left some of their plowed fields fallow, or unplanted. This way, they could store a year's moisture in the ground. The following year, the farmers alternated fields, planting the ones they had left fallow and resting the fields just harvested. Using this system, they had to plow under far more acreage than they intended to plant each year.

Fallowing was made much easier by the gasoline-powered tractor and the **one-way disk plow**. The one-way disk plow did not cut as deep into the earth as the old moldboard plow it replaced. Because of this, it broke the soil much more easily and quickly. Bright metal disks, polished by the soil, sliced through the earth and pulverized the clods of dirt.

Plowing became so easy that farmers who owned tractors continued disking the bare, fallow fields all summer long to rid them of weeds. They were proud of their smooth, tidy fields. The farmers did not realize that they were leaving large areas of loose topsoil vulnerable to the wind.

Just as tractors were replacing teams of draft animals in the fields, trucks began to replace animals for hauling the harvested crop to grain elevators for storage. When a combination harvester-thresher, known as the **combine**, was perfected in the early 1930s, farming on the Great Plains became thoroughly mechanized. Using the new combine, three people could now do the work of twenty.

Plains farmers who could afford to buy the new machines plowed under more grassland to plant larger crops. But an abundance of wheat during the late 1920s caused the market price to fall. The big farm owners simply bought more machines, plowed under more grassland, and harvested more wheat.

By selling in such large volume, they continued to make a profit, even at the lower prices. However, the small farmers could rarely afford the new machines, and their harvest seemed puny by comparison. Forced to sell their wheat at lower prices, they could no longer support their families.

Often these small farmers sold out to the big farm owners. Gradually, small farms were replaced by bigger and bigger farms. Some were as large as 50 square miles (80 square kilometers). These agricultural factories, as they became known, contained thousands of acres of wheat and corn.

But wheat and corn wither and die during prolonged dry weather, and with less grassland available, cattle overgraze on what remains. Overgrazed grasslands, like the fields of shallow-rooted wheat and corn, are also vulnerable to drought. A plains sheepherder once expressed the importance of the wild grasses with great precision:

> *Grass is what counts. It's what saves us all—far as we get saved....Grass is what holds the earth together.*

By the 1930s, over thirty million acres of the Dust Bowl—one-third of the region—had been stripped of its grassland. Then came the dry weather. And the winds began to blow.

During the Depression, many sharecroppers lived in rundown shacks that offered little comfort or protection from harsh plains weather.

While dust storms were beginning to devastate croplands of the southern plains, the **Great Depression** was having a similar effect on the nation's economy. An economic depression is characterized by a scarcity of goods and money, low prices, and mass unemployment. The Great Depression included all of these and more. Economists and historians still disagree over exactly what caused it, but it began shortly after the Stockmarket Crash of 1929.

Lasting throughout the thirties, the Great Depression occurred almost simultaneously with the Dust Bowl. Together they combined to cripple the American economy. Banks closed, factories were vacated, and machines went untended. In the big cities, hungry men and women stood in lines that stretched for several blocks, just to get a free bowl of soup. The more desperate sifted through garbage cans in back alleys. They had to compete with rats, stray dogs, and alley cats for rotting fruit, meat left on a bone, or a half-eaten sandwich.

Very few southern plains residents went hungry during the Depression—although their meals were often coated with dust. Even while drought and dust storms destroyed their wheat crops, most farm families managed to raise a flock of chickens, a few milk cows, and perhaps a pig or two. They stocked their pantries and storm cellars with butter, cheese, and eggs, along with preserved fruits and vegetables from their backyard garden. Whatever was left over they sold in town.

Some thrifty Dust Bowl families kept

their monthly food bills as low as ten dollars. The small amount they spent each month usually went toward items they could not produce at home, *staples* like flour, coffee, and salt. They scrimped and saved, all the while waiting for one good rain.

Many Dust Bowl wheat farmers were stubborn optimists, waiting for a soil-saving rain that never came. Many refused to admit that the southern plains had become a disaster area, even after drought and dust had destroyed one wheat crop after another. To do so meant admitting defeat, giving up their faith that the land would provide. Instead, they borrowed money to buy more land and plant more wheat. But crops continued to fail, and debts piled up.

Meanwhile, the drought had passed in the midwestern and southern states, and farmers there began turning out more wheat, corn, cotton, and hogs than people were able or willing to buy. This sudden surplus of farm products forced market prices to fall even further. Soon farmers throughout the U.S. were selling their products for less than what it cost to produce them. Nowhere, though, were farming conditions worse than in the Dust Bowl.

While dust storms and the Great Depression continued, many small farmers on the southern plains had to borrow money from local banks just to survive from day to day. But money was scarce, and the banks had to tighten their restrictions on loans. As a result, many debt-ridden farmers had to *mortgage* their farms.

Farmers who mortgaged their farms transferred title of ownership to the bank in exchange for a loan. The bank became

the legal owner of the farm, until the loan was repaid with interest. This arrangement was fine, as long as the farmer could pay back the loan on time. But many could not. When that happened, the banks had the right to *foreclose*, or take possession of the farmer's property. Often they took a family's house, fields, livestock, and machinery, leaving the family without the means to make a living.

Naturally, farmers felt increasingly bitter toward the bankers as they witnessed friends and neighbors losing their land and homes. Such was the case in the Cookson Hills region of eastern Oklahoma, the birthplace of Charles Arthur Floyd. Although he began as a Cookson Hills farmer, Floyd became known to the nation as Pretty Boy Floyd, a daring bank robber and the machine gun murderer in the famous Kansas City Massacre. In spite of his criminal activity, Pretty Boy Floyd was a folk hero to many Americans during the Depression.

When Pretty Boy Floyd robbed a bank, what people applauded was his defiance of the wealthy. Some even interpreted the murders he committed as acts of self defense. Romantic stories and songs about bandit-heroes who robbed from the rich and gave to the poor made this easier to do. Dust Bowl farmers identified with the bandits as downtrodden people like themselves, finally getting back what had been unfairly taken from them.

Pretty Boy Floyd was not the only outlaw-hero of the Dust Bowl. Another pair of Dust Bowl bandits was Bonnie Parker and Clyde Barrow, whose two-year spree of jail breaks and petty robberies left a dozen men dead. Their wild getaways and the sleazy, posed photographs they left behind for reporters created a romantic legend. When Bonnie and Clyde were shot down at a roadblock ambush by a posse of Texas Rangers, many law-abiding citizens mourned their death. Some people even idolized these bandits as folk heroes.

What would cause people to identify with bank robbers and ruthless murderers? Were depression era values so different from the ones we hold today? Certainly, the image of banks and bankers during the thirties was different. Debt-ridden Dust Bowl farmers and the jobless masses of the thirties perceived bankers and other big money makers as heartless symbols of greed and evil.

Indeed, bankers became very unpopular people during the Great Depression. This perception, however, was a result of the way victims of the Dust Bowl and the Great Depression perceived themselves. At first the farmers could not believe their misfortune. Hard-

PRETTY BOY FLOYD: DUST BOWL BANDIT

In 1930, while hiding out in Kansas City, Pretty Boy Floyd robbed a string of banks and killed five men, including three policemen. He was sentenced to fifteen years, but he escaped on the way to prison and fled home to the Cookson Hills.

In less than three months, he robbed eight Oklahoma banks. Often Floyd ripped up farm mortgages held by the banks he robbed, earning him the nickname "Robin Hood of the Cookson Hills." The farmers in this region viewed bankers as their enemies and Floyd as one of their own. They hid him and protected him from investigating lawmen.

On June 17, 1933, four officers and a prisoner were killed in the Kansas City train station by a machine gun-wielding murderer and his accomplice. The crime became known as the Kansas City Massacre, and lawmen and local newspapers claimed Pretty Boy Floyd was the killer. Sixteen months later, FBI agents tracked him to a field in the Ohio countryside. Floyd ran again, but this time they gunned him down. Not yet thirty-four, Pretty Boy Floyd was dead.

working men and women, many who for years had farmed, owned their own businesses, or held steady jobs, suddenly found themselves broke and unemployed. They felt somehow they had failed, and many were ashamed.

As the weeks of grinding poverty became months, Dust Bowl farmers asked for assistance from the new federal agencies established by President Franklin Roosevelt. Their shame grew as federal officials told them how to farm and which crops to plant. Other government officials told them how to manage their money and even how to plan their meals. Yet as more and more people found themselves in the same circumstances, they began to believe that the failure was not their own, but had been caused by something bigger.

Many people in the cities blamed big business for their difficulties. At first, Dust Bowl farmers blamed the weather. Then they blamed the banks for refusing to loan them money and the government for not putting pressure on the banks. They also complained that officials from federal agencies advised them to use farming methods that slowed them down and reduced their profit.

Whomever they blamed, Dust Bowl and Depression victims believed that they had been treated unfairly by the American system. Many felt that government was controlled by the wealthy and the only way to beat the system was by breaking the laws. They knew it was wrong to steal, but as they saw it, the banks had stolen their land, their machinery, and their livelihood.

Three
The Dirty Thirties

> *To the red country and part of the grey country of Oklahoma the last rains came gently, and they did not cut the scarred earth.*

So begins John Steinbeck's Pulitzer Prize-winning novel *The Grapes of Wrath*. John Steinbeck was an important American writer. Some of his other novels are *The Red Pony*, *Tortilla Flat*, *Of Mice and Men*, *Cannery Row*, and *East of Eden*. His best books are about common but memorable working class people and their relationship to the land, as in *The Grapes of Wrath*. Although the novel is classified as fiction, Steinbeck's account of the Dust Bowl and its survivors is remarkably authentic. Here, then, is his description of the sun-baked southern plains region that became the Dust Bowl of the 1930s:

> *In the roads where the teams moved, where the wheels milled the ground and the hooves of the horses beat the ground, the dirt crust broke and the dust formed. Every moving thing lifted the dust into the air; a walking man lifted a thin layer as high as his waist, and a wagon lifted the dust as high as the fence tops, and an automobile boiled a cloud behind it. The dust was long in settling back again.*

Steinbeck goes on to describe how the usual summer rain clouds, blowing northward out of the gulf, scattered only a few sprinkles over the southern plains. Then the sun burned in the sky, and the wind began to blow:

> *A gentle wind followed the rain clouds, driving them on northward.... A day went by and the wind increased, steady, unbroken by gusts. The dust from the roads fluffed up and spread out and fell on the weeds beside the fields, and fell into the fields a little way. Now the wind grew strong and hard and it worked at the rain crust in the cornfields. Little by little the sky was darkened by the mixing dust, and the wind felt over the earth, loosened the dust, and carried it away.*
>
> *The wind grew stronger. The rain crust broke and the dust lifted up out of the fields and drove grey plumes into the air like sluggish smoke.*

All day and night the wind blew. Wind-blown dust from the fields made it difficult to breathe. When morning came, the sun shone so dimly through the dust-blackened sky that it seemed like sundown, and at midday it looked the same. The dusky light soon faded to total darkness:

> *When the night came again it was black night, for the stars could not pierce the dust, and the window lights could not even spread beyond their own yards. Now the dust was evenly mixed with the air.... Houses were shut tight, and cloth wedged around doors and windows, but the dust came in so thinly that it could not be seen in the air, and it settled like pollen on the chairs and tables, on the dishes. The people brushed it from their shoulders. Little lines of dust lay at the door sills.*

Dust storms on the horizon were a frightening sight.

Kansas State Historical Society

Sometime during the night, the wind moved on, and an eerie silence followed its departure. People awakened to the silence, longing for the light and clamor of day. But the dawn light was a weak light, and the sound of roosters crowing carried faintly on the dust-filled air:

> *In the morning the dust hung like fog, and the sun was as red as ripe new blood. All day the dust sifted down from the sky, and the next day it sifted down. An even blanket covered the earth. It settled on the corn, piled up on the tops of the fence posts, piled up on the wires; it settled on roofs, blanketed the weeds and trees.*

The Grapes of Wrath was a sensational best-seller, dramatically increasing people's awareness of the Dust Bowl and its victims. Many other writers, painters, and photographers also came to the Dust Bowl to dramatize the plight of drought-stricken farmers. Some of these were employed by the federal government. For example, the **FSA**, or Farm Securities Administration, an agency established by President Roosevelt to help struggling farmers, assembled a group of talented photographers and sent them out to document the Dust Bowl tragedy and its many victims.

As public attention focused on the dust storms, plains men and women found themselves taking a defensive position. Dust Bowl businessmen, some who were farmers themselves, resented the manner in which Steinbeck and others depicted their native region. Dust Bowl bankers and realtors objected to photographers from the FSA collecting pictures of the destroyed landscape and despairing victims. They were worried that labeling the southern plains a disaster area would frighten away potential investors. Most insisted that it was only

Loose soil piled in drifts halfway up the sides of one-story shacks.

a temporary local problem, one that would resolve itself in time. "Drought and wind have to end sometime," they said. "One good rain will put an end to the dust."

But the rain never came, and there was no escaping the dust. It was everywhere—in the cupboards and clothes closets, coating the walls, carpets, and furniture. It was on the food people ate and in the water they drank, and it grated like sand against their teeth. They taped shut the cracks around their doors and windows or stuffed them with oiled rags to keep the dust out. Nothing worked. At night people slept with washrags over their noses, and they did not move for fear of disturbing the dust that had settled on their blankets.

The blowing dust triggered serious **_respiratory_** problems for many residents of the southern plains, particularly infants and the elderly. Those who already suffered from asthma, bronchitis, or tuberculosis saw their conditions worsen. A strange **_bronchial_** disease labeled **_dust pneumonia_** suddenly emerged on the plains. Those afflicted coughed up clots of mud and complained of burning, bloodshot eyes and inflamed nostrils. The mysterious disease became so widespread that the Red Cross set up several emergency hospitals on the southern plains. Most Dust Bowl doctors argued that the new pneumonia was not caused by blowing dust, but they were unable to say what had caused it.

A discouraged Dust Bowl farmer scans the bare, eroded fields.

Meanwhile the dust continued to blow. Dust storms blew from all directions with incredible force, shaking the wooden frames of the sturdiest farmhouses with winds up to 70 miles per hour (112.7 kilometers per hour).

In several places, the unrelenting wind laid bare tools and **relics** left by earlier inhabitants of the southern plains. Farmers discovered Indian arrowheads, Spanish stirrups, pioneer wagon wheels and branding irons. In other places, wind stripped away the topsoil to expose a rocklike layer of **hardpan**, soil in which neither wild grass nor a farmer's crops could put down roots.

The worst of these storms traveled phenomenal distances. Dust Bowl dirt was carried as far away as the gulf coast of Texas and to cities in the eastern United States. It muddied the snow-covered hills of the New Hampshire countryside and hung like smoke in the skies above New York, Boston, and Washington DC. It even powdered the decks of oceangoing ships 300 miles (483 kilometers) off the Atlantic Coast.

Some people believed the dust storms were the heaven-sent punishment of a wrathful God. They prayed for deliverance, read the Bible, and waited for the Day of Judgment. On Sunday April 14, 1935, many were convinced that day had finally come.

DUST BOWL HUMOR

Despite the terrible dust storms raging all around them, residents of the southern plains refused to surrender their sense of humor. One Dust Bowl joke popular during the thirties went as follows:

A tourist driving along the highway stopped to pick up a ten-gallon hat that he saw perched on a roadside sand dune. Lifting the hat, he uncovered a head.

"Good lord!" exclaimed the startled tourist. "Let me help you!"

"Naw, it's all right," said the man under the hat.

"At least let me give you a ride into town," urged the tourist.

"Thanks," said the man under the hat, "but I can make it on my own. I'm on a horse."

Woody Guthrie, one of America's finest folksingers and songwriters, was born in Oklahoma. As a young man he experienced the dust storms of the 1930s. The words from his song, "Dust Storm Disaster," give us some idea of the horror and awe felt by those who were there on that April day in 1935, a day that became known as Black Sunday:

On the 14th day of April of 1935,
There struck the worst of dust storms
That ever filled the sky.
It fell across our city
Like a curtain of black rolled down
We thought it was our judgment
We thought it was our doom.

Arthur Rothstein, Dover Publications, Inc.

Many farmers abandoned their plows in the fields. Wind and sand soon made them part of the landscape.

That Sunday morning in April began warm as summer, and the wide prairie sky at midday was a bright blue. But within a few hours, temperatures in some areas of the plains had plunged fifty degrees. Through the rapidly cooling air flew flocks of frightened birds, twittering anxiously as they fled from the northern sky. Without warning, a monstrous cloud appeared behind the birds. Dark as a thunderhead and boiling with dust, it rose from the boundless prairie horizon high into the sky, rolling across the southern plains toward the Gulf of Mexico.

The blowing dust was so thick on Black Sunday that motorists peering through their windshields could not even see the hood ornaments on their own vehicles. Abandoning their cars, panic stricken travelers stumbled blindly through the swirling dust toward fences bordering the roadside. Using the fence wire to guide them, they tore their flesh on the barbs as they traced it, hand over hand, to the nearest farmhouse.

Cattle were also blinded by the blowing dust, and some suffocated as it clogged their lungs. Those that survived ground their teeth to the gums chewing the grit-covered grass. A murky film of dust settled on the surface of the shallow prairie rivers, even killing fish in some places. Fence posts and farm machinery were completely covered over. In some areas, only the rooftop of the smaller outbuildings protruded above the sand dunes.

Before and after Black Sunday, journalists during the 1930s wrote about the devastation caused by dust storms on the southern plains. George Greenfield of *The New York Times*, while a passenger on the Union Pacific Railroad, observed the Kansas landscape after a black blizzard had struck. He wrote this description of what he saw:

> *Today I have seen the cold hand of death on what was one of the great bread-baskets of the nation… a lost people living in a lost land.*

And Albert Law, a local southern plains reporter, gave a far more detailed account of the scene:

> *Not a blade of grass in Cimarron County, Oklahoma; cattle dying there on the range… ninety per cent of the poultry dead because of sand storms; sixty cattle dying Friday afternoon between Guymon and Liberal from some disease induced by the dust—humans suffering from dust fever—milk cows going dry, turned into pasture to starve, hogs in such pitiable shape that buyers will not have them… no wheat in Hartley County… cattle facing starvation… other Panhandle counties with one-third their population on charity or relief work; ninety percent of farmers in most counties have to use crop loans, and continued drought forcing many of them to use the money for food, clothes, medicine, shelter.*

But it was Robert Geiger, a reporter for the Associated Press, who gave the Dust Bowl its name. He personally witnessed Black Sunday, and in a routine newspaper article, Geiger renamed the southern plains for his and future generations.

Black Sunday, April 14, 1935

Kansas State Historical Society

Within a few days, his report was read by people all over the country:

> *Three little words, achingly familiar on a western farmer's tongue, rule life in the dust bowl of the continent: if it rains.*

Monster dust storms like the one occurring on Black Sunday eroded the determination of all but the hardiest Dust Bowl residents. The storms were especially defeating to sharecroppers unable to pay their rent and to the owners of mortgaged farms unable to pay back their loans. "Baked-out, blown-out, and broke" became a familiar expression. Many of these failed farmers packed what they could carry in their cars and migrated to California, leaving land, buildings, and machinery to their creditors.

Four
Dust Bowl Orphans

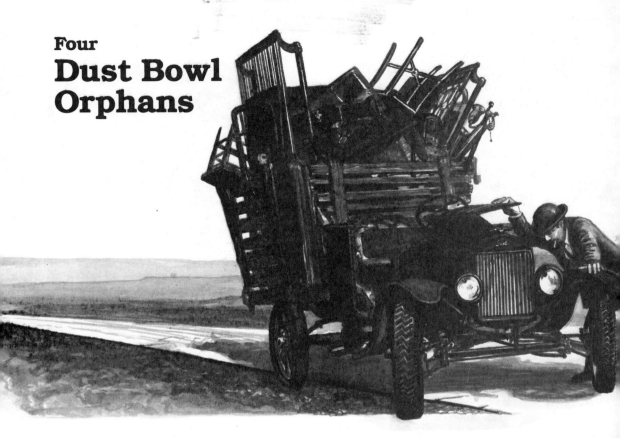

Southern plains farmers defeated by the dust storms were certain that they would find work in California. Many went in response to local newspaper advertisements assuring them that migrant workers were needed in the fields and orchards of the Golden State. The crops in California required little attention except during harvest time, so there was a massive labor force made up of wandering farm workers.

But as the farmers loaded their dilapidated old cars with their favorite belongings and set out for California, they also believed that they would find something more. They did not consider themselves migrant workers, forever following the harvests from season to season. If someone had asked them, they would have stated it in simple terms "We're just farmin' folks lookin' to wor our piece of land."

In California, they hoped to recreat the farms they had lost to drought an wind. With this unshakable dream, the left the Dust Bowl and steered thei wheezing jalopies west along Route 66 As they headed over the mountains an across the desert, the dust seemed t be following them. Dust from the Nev Mexico highlands colored their cars pinl and dust from the cactus country o Arizona colored the cars gray.

With household belongings tied t the roof and **running boards**, the dus covered jalopies became a familiar sigh sputtering down the highway or broker down along the roadside. Other moto ists traveling Route 66 saw migrants eating their lunch in the shade of roadside billboards while they waited for their car radiators to stop steaming so they could fill them with water. People saw the migrants in roadside diners, buying milk for their children.

In gas stations along the highway, motorists witnessed the Dust Bowl refugees digging into their purses or the pockets of their overalls to find enough money to pay for gas and oil.

At night they pulled off the road wherever they saw the campfires of other migrant families following the great cross-country highway to California. In *The Grapes of Wrath*, John Steinbeck describes the spirit of togetherness typical of these migrant families:

> And [new] worlds were built in the evening. The people, moving in from the highways, made them with their tents and their hearts and their brains.
>
> In the morning the tents came down, the canvas was folded, the tent poles tied along the running-board, the beds put in place on the cars, the pots in their places. And as the families moved westward, the technique of building up a home in the evening and tearing it down with the morning light became fixed; so that the folded tent was packed in one place, the cooking pots counted in their box. And as the cars moved westward, each member of the family grew into his proper place, grew into his duties; so that each member, old and young, had his place in the car; so that in the weary, hot evenings, when the cars pulled into the camping places, each member had his duty and went to it without instruction: children to gather wood, to carry water; men to pitch the tents and bring down the beds; women to cook the supper and to watch while the family fed.

At last they reached California—the golden land, the promised land. But in California, the people called them **Okies**. Although more Dust Bowl migrants came from Oklahoma than from any other state, many came from Texas, New Mexico, Kansas, and Colorado, too. Yet no matter where they came from, if they were poor, white, and rural, then they were Okies as far as Californians were concerned. And from the moment of their arrival, they were made to feel unwelcome.

Where the major highways entered southern California, the Los Angeles police set up illegal roadblocks, turning away migrants without money or proof of employment. But the Okies came anyway, stealing past the blockades by night on dirt backroads.

Russell Lee, Library of Congress LC-USF34-33418

Okie camping on the route west.

Thousands of Dust Bowl refugees fled to California during the 1930s, seeking employment as farm laborers. California had long held its reputation as a virtual Garden of Eden—a region where the soil was unbelievably rich, the weather was mild, and crops were harvested year-round. By 1930, California was turning out nearly two hundred different farm products, and agriculture was its major industry.

Although small farms existed in California, most of the farmland in the state was divided into large **corporate farms**. Crops grown on these huge farms had to be harvested quickly and by hand. Because of this, California growers depended on the large force of cheap migrant labor. Most of these migrant workers came from Mexico. Once the crops were harvested, the Mexicans returned to their native country or to **barrios**, the Mexican communities adjoining the large California cities.

But as the Great Depression began in the 1930s, growers were seeking a new source of cheap labor. There were two reasons for this. First, California farm production was slowed by the depression. When Mexican migrant workers saw the dwindling number of available jobs, many of them panicked and returned to their homeland. Secondly, a 1929 immigration restriction temporarily halted the entry of more Mexicans into California.

There were still more workers than there were jobs available in California, but the growers wanted a bigger labor supply to keep wages low. Some unscrupulous growers placed advertisements in Dust Bowl area newspapers inviting jobless plains farmers to come west and pick crops. Most often, the advertisements were for jobs that did not really exist.

Arriving in California without the money to buy or rent a place to live, many of these men and women from the southern plains had no choice but to camp in the fields. They built their camps, which became known as **ditchbank camps**, along the banks of the irrigation ditches.

Most of the Okies who came to California found that the jobs they sought were already taken. For every new job that opened up, there were two or three men or women waiting to grab it. Desperate for work, they crowded each other out of steady employment. The lucky ones landed jobs picking vegetables or fruit. But the harvest seasons were short, and there was little work in between.

While looking for work, the unemployed Okies formed their own settlements in the fields. In the best of these ditchbank camps, conditions were unsanitary. The worst of the camps were so dirty they became breeding grounds for illness and disease. Pure drinking water was simply unavailable. Rusty tin cans occasionally served as cooking pots, and the ditches served as toilets. Smallpox epidemics raged throughout these wretched camps. Occasional outbreaks of typhoid, tuberculosis, malaria, and pneumonia also plagued the Okies.

MIGRANT MOTHER

American photographer Dorothea Lange was driving home after completing an assignment for the FSA photographing the migrant camps in California's great central valley. She was headed for San Francisco alone when she happened to pass a makeshift sign that read, Pea-Pickers Camp.

Arriving at the ditchbank migrant camp, she grabbed her camera and stepped out of her car into the rain and mud. Lange described what happened next:

I saw and approached the hungry and desperate mother, as if drawn by a magnet. . . . She told me her age, that she was thirty-two. She said that they had been living on frozen vegetables from the surrounding fields, and birds that the children killed. She had just sold the tires from her car to buy food. There she sat in the lean-to tent with her children huddled around her, and seemed to know that my pictures might help her, and so she helped me. There was a sort of equality about it.

This great American photograph became known as "Migrant Mother." Even today, it is frequently reproduced in books, magazines, and newspapers and is shown in exhibitions all over the world.

Dorothea Lange, Library of Congress LC-USF34-9058

California's "Okie problem" became a national scandal. The federal government finally responded by building migrant camps in some of the agricultural areas. A marked improvement over the rag towns, as some called the ditch-bank camps, the federal camps provided visiting nurses and were equipped with running water, showers, and toilets.

Although living conditions in the federal camps were primitive, the Okies were determined to make the best of them. They established self-governing committees and elected their own officers. The sanitary units were regularly cleaned and the grounds kept free of litter. They helped each other by exchanging job information, such as who was hiring and when.

The young children of employed mothers were supervised by women who stayed home. For entertainment, every camp had its fiddlers, banjo players, and guitar pickers who played for dances on Saturday nights. It was not the place they had come west hoping to find, but at least the government-built camps offered the Okies a clean, safe shelter where they could restore their health and rebuild their shattered dreams. Still, even those who found steady work were scorned by the established communities.

In the schools, California children mocked the migrant pupils for their "Okie drawls," and teachers showed little patience with their lack of education. Ministers of some established community churches discouraged Okies from attending services. One minister explained that they did not dress well enough to feel comfortable in his church, and suggested they attend fundamentalist tent revivals instead. "These

churches are more like their homes," he said. "They can live in a tent and feel comfortable there."

The Okies who fled the dust storms were seeking a new life on their own piece of land. Instead, they encountered the same kinds of discrimination often experienced by other minorities. The typical attitude among Californians was reflected in a sign that appeared in the lobby of a San Joaquin Valley theater: "Negroes and Okies Upstairs."

Rather than face this kind of prejudice, many Dust Bowl refugees settled on the outskirts of agricultural towns. Ernie Pyle, a journalist, described one of these Okie settlements:

But many Californians felt that the Okies had brought their problems on themselves. Others simply did not want the migrants settling in their state. President Roosevelt received this letter from a California woman:

They say you can go into a big settlement…and you can judge by a man's place to the very month how long he has been here.…If he's living in a tent or trailer, he's been here for less than six months. If a family is in a garage on the back of a lot, they've been here more than six months. If the garage now houses the car, and the family is in a two-room shack in the front of the lot, they've been here more than a year. And if the house has expanded and living is fairly decent, they've been here for more than two years.

Okies were the victims of a farming culture and economic system beyond their control. They tolerated poverty and filth only when they had no other choice.

A Federal migratory camp is being established adjacent to my property at Porterville, Tulare County, California.

Knowing the character of migrants from my experience in dealing with them, I object to these hordes of degenerates being located at my very door.

These "sharecroppers" are not a noble people looking for a home and seeking an education for their children. They are unprincipled degenerates looking for something for nothing.

The fact that they are leaving their native land unfit for human habitation is not surprising. Their ignorance and maliciousness in caring for trees, crops, vines, and the land is such that California will be ruined if farming is left to them.

Please do not put these vile people at my door to depreciate my property and to loot my ranch.

Five
The New Deal

In 1932, Franklin Delano Roosevelt had succeeded the unpopular Herbert Hoover as president of the United States. Under his leadership, the Democratic party promised Americans a "new deal" that would restrain the few who were financially powerful and provide a better life for the nation's poor. For this reason, the Roosevelt administration became known as the New Deal.

To resolve the many problems arising from the Dust Bowl and the Great Depression, New Deal administrators created a number of so-called "alphabet agencies" during the 1930s. But finding solutions that worked for Dust Bowl farmers was not easy. These administrators, often working out of offices in Washington DC, were far removed from blowing dust and dying crops on the southern plains.

Plans that looked good on paper did not always produce the desired results. For example, New Dealers tried to reverse the plunging market price of farm products by forming the Agricultural Adjustment Administration, or **AAA**. The AAA introduced "planned scarcity," through which it hoped to raise prices by limiting the amount of farm products brought to market. Farmers were federally **subsidized**, or paid by the U.S. government, to cultivate fewer acres and to destroy a portion of their livestock. Under this policy, 6 million piglets and 200 thousand sows were slaughtered, and 10 million acres of cotton were plowed under.

If planned scarcity seems like a terrible waste to us now, imagine how it seemed during the disastrous thirties, when small farm owners and sharecroppers were barely surviving on the southern plains. They watched as federal workers came to the big ranches and shot the surplus cattle. On big corporate farms, they saw wheat left unharvested in the fields. They saw warehouses filled with rotting grain. At the same time, the small farms had no surplus livestock to slaughter, no surplus wheat to waste. They were barely producing enough to support themselves and their families. To them, the planned scarcity program made no sense. As a result, many farmers began to distrust all federal agencies.

Sharecroppers suffered the most. Large landowners received federal money for leaving their fields uncultivated. That meant they did not need as many tenant farmers. Unintentionally, the AAA was encouraging large landowners of the southern plains to evict their tenants.

PRESIDENT FRANKLIN ROOSEVELT

Franklin Delano Roosevelt, also known as FDR, was president of the United States from 1933 through 1944. FDR was born into a prominent political family. Teddy Roosevelt, a cousin, had served as president from 1901 to 1909. FDR's wife, Eleanor, was also a distant cousin. Many people believe she was the finest first lady America has ever had.

Despite his wealth and aristocratic background, FDR considered himself a champion of the underdog. His leadership during a difficult period in American history earned him the trust of most Americans. Although he died in 1945 while still president, his twelve years in office is the longest of any American president. Roosevelt is the only president ever to have been elected to four consecutive terms.

What happened to sharecroppers as a result of the AAA's federal subsidy program is best explained by this Oklahoma landowner:

I let 'em all go. In '34 I had I reckon four renters (sharecroppers) and I didn't make anything. I bought tractors on the money the government give me and got shet o' (got rid of) my renters. You'll find it all over the country thataway. I did everything the government said—except keep my renters. The renters have been having it this way ever since the government come in. They've got their choice— California or WPA.

THE FSA PHOTOGRAPHERS

Determined to counteract its critics, the FSA's Information Division assembled a group of talented photographers. They were sent out to document the Dust Bowl tragedy and the miserable conditions of migrants camped beside the irrigation ditches bordering California farms.

The photo above by Dorothea Lange is one example of the striking images recorded by FSA photographers. Regardless of its shortcomings, the FSA did accomplish something exceptionally worthwhile. The vivid images of Depression America and the Dust Bowl have become a national historical treasure.

"California or WPA." Unfortunately, displaced farmers on the southern plains had few other alternatives. There were many who mistakenly believed that they would find better conditions in the fields and orchards of California. Not all of the displaced farmers left, however. Some went to work for the Works Progress Administration, commonly called the WPA. Typically, they hired out as laborers on construction projects improving playgrounds, schools, hospitals, roads, and airfields.

Often, though, working for the WPA was not much better than signing up for relief, or financial assistance from the government. The pay was pitiful (thirty cents an hour) and a worker's weekly hours were purposely kept short. The low wages were intended to encourage WPA workers to find private employment as soon as possible.

Neither the AAA nor the WPA was doing much to help sharecroppers and small farmers, so the New Dealers created another federal agency, the Farm Security Administration, or FSA. Officials from the FSA encouraged unsuccessful farmers to **diversify**, or vary, their farm products. Instead of relying solely on a wheat crop, participating farmers could borrow enough money from the FSA to seed some of their fields with grass and buy a few cows to start a small herd of cattle. The FSA also encouraged the production of more butter, cream, and eggs. Besides providing food for the farmer's family, these dairy and poultry products required only a small investment and could be sold for a profit.

The FSA made a sincere attempt to aid small farmers on the southern plains. Unfortunately, with such a tangle of federal agencies, those farmers who needed the most help often received the least. The larger, prosperous landowners, who were already receiving substantial federal subsidies from the AAA, were eager to get their hands on more. They resented the FSA because they believed that aiding smaller farmers was a waste of money, and they had powerful friends in government who agreed with them. As a result, the FSA, which had to compete with the AAA and other federal agencies for funds, was under-financed and understaffed.

While the FSA and other agencies were trying to improve the farmers' plight, scientists with yet another federal agency, the **SCS**, or Soil Conservation Service, began to probe for the causes of their problems. These scientists were *agronomists*, experts in crop production and soil management. They realized that to heal the wind-eroded land and make it produce, they had to convince Dust Bowl farmers to use scientific methods.

The agronomists took aerial photographs of the entire Dust Bowl region. They used the photos to draw maps showing the various soil types found in each county. They also analyzed the wind and water erosion that had occurred throughout the Dust Bowl. Based on the data they had collected, the agronomists recommended farming methods that best suited the soil and erosion factors of a given area.

Respect the land and protect the soil, they told the farmers, and it would pay off in better production. The agronomists' advice was certain to pay off in the long run, but it was of no use to farmers who were in immediate danger of losing their land.

None of the federal agencies of the New Deal could resolve all of America's economic and social problems. However, their advice and financial assistance helped many survive the Great Depression. Equally important, most Americans saw that President Roosevelt genuinely cared about them

CONTROLLING WIND AND WATER EROSION

Agronomists encouraged *contour plowing* on hills to reduce both wind erosion and water runoff.

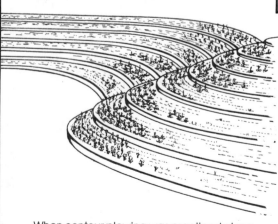

When contour plowing was practiced along with *terracing*, they said, the stair-stepped rows greatly increased the soil's ability to absorb water.

Agronomists also recommended the planting of *shelter belts* to slow the force of the wind and cool the surrounding area. This helps offset the effects of heat and drought on crops.

A NATURAL BALANCE

According to *ecologists*, every region of the world has an *ecosystem*, or a community of living *organisms*. This community can only continue if it is in a state of *equilibrium*, or natural balance.

This means plants must be sufficient to provide food for *herbivores*, the animals which eat only plants. The herbivores, in turn, must be numerous enough to withstand the attacks of predators, yet not so numerous that they overgraze the plants. And *carnivores*, or meat eaters, cannot become too plentiful for their food supply, the herbivores, or plant eaters. Once this equilibrium is established, relationships within the community stabilize and the organisms can remain healthy.

and their difficulties. At the very least, FDR's inspiring leadership renewed their courage and gave them hope.

But neither the caring president nor his New Deal administrators alone brought an end to the Great Depression. Ironically, that came as a direct result of an even greater disaster—the Second World War. When the United States entered the war in 1941, the massive war effort put most Americans to work. Many enlisted in the military. Others took jobs providing the weapons, ammunition, machinery and supplies needed to sustain the military.

The economic revival was contagious, spreading to private industry as well, until a slumbering American economy stirred and awakened. Very quickly, it began to gather momentum. At last, after twelve agonizing years, the Great Depression was over.

Coincidentally, 1941 was also the year the drought ended and dust storms died down on the southern plains. As the rains fell and sturdy new shoots of corn and wheat filled their fields, Dust Bowl farmers rejoiced. When their first good harvest in a decade came that summer, Dust Bowl farmers found an eager market waiting for their products.

The Dust Bowl disaster had caused tremendous hardships, but it also forced farmers to learn better methods of dry land farming. This drew attention to the new science of *ecology*. Ecologists study how various plants and animals interact in their environment.

The ecologists explained how nature maintains an *equilibrium*, or natural balance, permitting the various *species* of plants and animals in a particular environment to survive. Such a harmonious balance, they thought, can be disturbed only by a change of climate or the invasion of new organisms.

HOW MONOCULTURE FARMING DISRUPTS THE BALANCE

Whenever a new organism appears in an ecosystem, it affects the entire system. **Monoculture** farming, or cultivating huge fields of a single crop, does just that.

For example, the millions of acres of wheat and corn on the southern plains have made permanent changes there. The wild grasses have disappeared, and so have many of the herbivores, such as buffalo, that fed on these grasses. The vast fields of wheat and corn have created a new ecosystem heavily populated by rabbits, mice, grasshoppers, and thousands of other insects that thrive on these plants.

Ecologists realized that the Dust Bowl could never be restored to the equilibrium it enjoyed before the homesteader invasion. Southern plains agriculture had demonstrated too great a potential for profit, so it was on the prairie to stay. Therefore, these scientists called for a new kind of plains equilibrium, one designed to benefit its dominating organism, the farmer.

They argued that modern agriculture could not continue to ignore the natural balance without causing serious damage. They pointed out that before white settlers came to the southern plains, the prairie had hosted a balanced community of grasses and wildlife. Even a man-made equilibrium, they insisted, had to follow nature's model.

Research was conducted on the various plains soils and recommendations were made. Scientists learned that dark, compact soils hold water well but absorb it so slowly that most is lost in runoff. In this soil, wheat can be raised in combination with a variety of agricultural products.

The light-colored, sandy soils quickly absorb rainwater, but they do not hold it well. These soils are subject to drought and are the first to blow in a windstorm. Sandy ground, suggested the ecologists, should be reseeded with wild grass to root the soil and should be used only for grazing.

No matter what kind of soil was being farmed, ecologists favored small farms supporting a variety of crops and livestock. They considered **monoculture farming**, or the cultivation of a single crop, ecologically unsound.

But southern plains farmers were more interested in economics than ecology. Using new farming methods and the constantly improving machinery, farmers planted and harvested their crops with greater speed and less labor. Bigger and better tractors dragged 42-foot-wide (12.6-meter-wide) plows through the soil. Throughout the forties, yields of corn and wheat steadily increased on the southern plains. Once again, large corporate farms became the trend, and suitcase farmers reappeared. Every good harvest gave the farmers greater confidence.

Yet as bigger harvests brought bigger profits, the farmers began to disregard warnings about wind erosion. They followed the advice of SCS scientists when it helped increase production and profit, but not when it slowed production or increased cost. Within a single decade after one of the greatest natural disasters in American history, southern plains farmers were behaving as if the Dust Bowl had never happened.

With characteristic optimism, they had plowed under another four million acres of grassland by the fall of 1946. And they planted almost all of these fields with wheat. When drought and windstorms returned to the region in 1952, the land was just as vulnerable as it had been twenty years before. Instead of the "dirty thirties," it was the "filthy fifties."

Although this second dust bowl lasted only five years instead of ten, it caused the same kind of devastation to the land. Dust storms made driving hazardous, cattle choked to death on inhaled dust, and cultivated fields were stripped of their topsoil. But once again the land recovered. And once again, farmers plowed under more grassland as they resumed their monoculture farming of wheat. In 1974, a three-year drought with accompanying windstorms again struck the southern plains. It was only an unpredictable change in weather that made this third dust bowl shorter and less destructive than the first two. And this same unpredictable weather makes the soil of the southern plains just as vulnerable to abusive farming today as it was during the thirties.

Six
In Harmony with the Land

The Dust Bowl of the 1930s was not just a natural disaster. It was an ecological disaster that began over a half-century earlier, when large numbers of white ranchers and farmers first came to the southern plains. There they found a level, fertile land that they believed would be ideal for raising cattle and crops. Ranching and farming methods introduced by these early settlers, and continued by those who came later, gradually upset the natural balance of plant and animal life.

When drought and dust storms struck the southern plains, decades of land abuse had already left the region vulnerable to extremes of weather. The disaster thus created will always be associated with the 1930s, but the story of how and why it happened began in the year 1866, when the southern plains was still an unspoiled grassland, more than sixty years before it became known as the Dust Bowl.

For thousands of years, wild grasses flourished on the prairie of the Great Plains in harmony with herbivores and **carnivores**. But when plains farmers broke the sod with their plows, they destroyed the firmly-rooted wild grasses and replaced them with **domesticated** varieties.

Lacking the extensive root system of wild grasses, domesticated grasses such as wheat and corn require regular rainfall or irrigation. Without water, they soon wither and die during prolonged dry weather.

Neither the extremes of weather, the vast herds of grazing buffaloes, nor the nations of predatory Indians could disturb the grassland's complex ecology. Yet, in the short span of fifty years, the homesteader invasion did just that. It eliminated both buffalo and Indian, while unrestricted plowing and overgrazing destroyed the grass.

Living grass holds the protective sod in place, and decaying grass is a valuable fertilizer. Planted crops such as wheat and corn do not hold or fertilize the soil. Instead, annual planting and harvesting of these domestic crops depletes, or exhausts, the soil, robbing it of minerals. At the same time, continued plowing leaves the soil at the mercy of strong winds.

Drought and winds have always plagued the southern plains, but until the 1930s there was never a Dust Bowl. Monoculture farming turned our nation's largest expanse of unspoiled grassland into field upon field of wheat and corn. Decades of overplowing and overgrazing have permanently altered the ecological balance, and very little native grass has been left to hold the soil. When future droughts descend on the region accompanied by windstorms, we can expect this destructive combination to produce more dust bowls.

Throughout history, land abuse has contributed to the downfall of flourishing civilizations. Three thousand years ago, seafaring **Phoenicians** delivered forty shiploads of timber to King Solomon of Israel for use in the temple at Jerusalem. Most of the timber came from cedar trees, highly valued for their durability and fragrant aroma. Before Phoenician woodcutters felled these trees, they were part of a dense forest known as the "Cedars of Lebanon." But today, what used to be a majestic cedar forest along the eastern coastline of the Mediterranean Sea is mostly bare rocky slopes.

The Mediterranean region provides other historical examples of land abuse. North African countries currently experiencing food shortages were once the major suppliers of grain, wine, and olives for the Roman Empire. Jordan and the barren Sinai peninsula make up an area that was called Canaan in biblical times. This biblical Canaan was so widely known for its fertile pastures and flourishing livestock that outsiders referred to it as the "land of milk and honey." Historians have yet to discover how this rich farmland declined to its present state, but land abuse probably contributed to the downfall.

Today, land abuse poses a serious problem worldwide. Approximately fifty million acres of the world's farmland is lost every year because of poor land management. As populations grow, farmers are forced to seek new areas for cultivation, even if these new areas are fragile environments subject to drought. Fifteen percent of the world's population now lives in arid or semiarid regions, and nearly eighty million of these people occupy lands suffering from soil erosion

caused by overgrazing and overplowing.

In Africa, the abuse of semiarid lands bordering the Sahara Desert has turned potentially good farmland into desert, a process known as **desertification**. Previously, traditional farming methods practiced in this region had benefitted the environment. African farmers wisely let their fields lie fallow for two or three years between plantings. During this fallow period, the natural vegetation renewed itself and enriched the soil. They left the native acacia trees untouched, so that the tree roots held the soil in place and added valuable nitrogen. Farmers also encouraged **nomadic** herders to graze their cattle and goats on the fallow fields, aware that the animals would supply even more fertilizer with their droppings.

Recently, however, African farmers have changed their traditional methods to meet the increased demand for food. Hoping to improve production, they began to keep their fields continually under cultivation.

Since fallow fields were no longer available, herders restricted their livestock to smaller pastures, which led to overgrazing. Today, African farmers are also chopping down the acacia trees to make plowing easier. Their continual cultivation is steadily robbing the soil of valuable minerals and organic matter. Farmers are forced to use artificial fertilizers. Gambling that larger yields would make up for the higher costs, these farmers plowed fields and planted them with more crops. But the increased need for expensive fertilizers often raised their expenses so high it eliminated profits entirely. When this happened, bankrupt farmers migrated to the cities in search of work. Like the failed farmers of the Dust Bowl, they left behind a barren land, stripped of vegetation and vulnerable to erosion by water or wind.

African farmers and herders are not the only ones guilty of land abuse. Deserts are expanding throughout the Middle East and Southwest Asia. On the South American continent, the central states of Argentina are fast becoming deserts, as is the semiarid tip of northeastern Brazil. In the United States, 10 percent of the farmland has already been affected by desertification, and another 20 percent is believed to be endangered.

Today, world population is nearly five billion. Demands for food and living space continue to increase at an alarming rate. Unfortunately, the cultivation of ecologically sensitive areas is necessary to meet these demands. And the damage that is done to the land now may not be noticeable for hundreds of years. By then, it may be too late to correct.

Ironically, much of the damage to the environment has resulted from attempts to meet increasing demands for food, clothing, and shelter. In supplying these human needs, we have reduced the population of wild animals. We have drained lakes and rivers and leveled entire forests. Meanwhile, deserts continue to spread into the world's grasslands.

Soil *conservationists* say farmers must find ways to meet worldwide food demands without disturbing the ecological balance. They have shown how contour plowing and terracing can decrease wind erosion and water runoff. Shelter belts break the wind and help cool the air, and small fields with a variety of crops and livestock cause less damage to the environment than vast fields of wheat or corn alone.

Wheat and corn are not only suscepible to drought, they seriously deplete the soil. At an agricultural experimental station in Kansas, Dr. Wes Jackson is working to establish a grain-bearing perennial to replace the domestic crops of wheat and corn. According to Dr. Jackson of the Land Institute, wild perennials "have evolved methods for dispersing seed, recycling minerals, building soil, . . . and even controlling weeds." If Dr. Jackson's experiments are successful, such a crop would provide a year-round ground cover and eliminate much of the plowing and planting cycle.

Research and experimentation continue, and new solutions are being proposed. But if these solutions require farmers to do more work for less money, they will not work. Farming is a business, and like every business, it cannot survive without profits. Farmers alone cannot bear the responsibility for protecting the environment. That responsibility belongs to everyone.

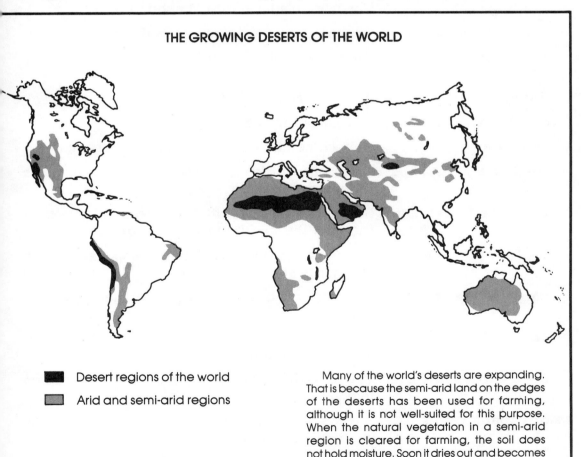

THE GROWING DESERTS OF THE WORLD

■ Desert regions of the world

▨ Arid and semi-arid regions

Many of the world's deserts are expanding. That is because the semi-arid land on the edges of the deserts has been used for farming, although it is not well-suited for this purpose. When the natural vegetation in a semi-arid region is cleared for farming, the soil does not hold moisture. Soon it dries out and becomes a desert.

Glossary

AAA . . . . Agricultural Adjustment Administration, an agency of the U.S. government.

agronomist . . . . [uh-**GRON**-o-mist] An expert in crop production and soil management.

annual . . . . A plant that dies after a single growing season.

arid . . . . Not having enough rainfall for many things to grow. A desert is arid.

barrio . . . . [**BAR**-ee-o] A Hispanic neighborhood.

binding deck . . . . The work platform on a Marsh Harvester.

black blizzard . . . . A severe dust storm characterized by a black cloud.

bronchial . . . . [**BRAWN**-key-ul] Relating to the two tubes leading to the lungs.

bumper crop . . . . A very large harvest.

carnivore . . . . A meat-eating animal.

combine . . . . A machine that threshes grain as it harvests it.

condense . . . . To become thicker or denser. For example, vapor condenses to form water.

conservationist . . . . . . Someone concerned with the protection and preservation of the world's natural resources.

contour plowing . . . . . Plowing along the natural lines of slopes and ridges in order to stop erosion.

corporate farm . . . . . . A large farm owned by a partnership of several people.

crankshaft . . . . A shaft driven by a piston in order to transfer up and down motion into circular motion.

desertification . . . . The transformation of marginally productive lands to desert.

ditchbank camp . . . . . . A camp located on the bank of a roadside ditch or an irrigation ditch and inhabited by refugees of the Dust Bowl and the Great Depression.

diversify . . . . To produce a variety of products.

domesticated . . . . Raised or cultivated for use by humans.

draft . . . . Used for hauling or pulling loads.

drought . . . . [**DROUT**] A prolonged period of dry weather.

dust pneumonia . . . . . . A respiratory infection believed to be caused by dust storms in the 1930s.

ecology . . . . The branch of science concerned with living things and their relationship to their environment.

ecosystem . . . . The community of all living things in a particular environment.

equilibrium . . . . [e-quill-**IB**-re-um] A state of balance.

erode . . . . To wear away the soil by water or wind.

fallow . . . . [**FAL**-o] Plowed but left unplanted during the growing season.

flatiron . . . . A non-electric iron in the shape of a triangle, used to press clothes.

foreclose . . . . A legal process that allows a creditor, such as a bank which holds rights to a property, to claim ownership.

FSA . . . . Farm Securities Administration, an agency of the U.S. government.

Great Depression . . . . . The period during the 1930s marked by a failing economy and rising unemployment.

hardpan . . . . The hard layer of earth below the topsoil.

herbivore . . . . [**HER**-buh-vore] A plant-eating animal.

humid . . . . Damp.

immigration . . . . The movement of people to a new country to live.

irrigate . . . . To supply cultivated plants with water by artificial means.

leach . . . . To rinse out of the soil, as with minerals and nutrients that drain out with rainwater or irrigation.

loess . . . . [**LESS**] An extremely fertile soil deposited by the wind.

Marsh Harvester . . . . . A harvesting machine in popular use at the beginning of the 1800s.

Mason jar . . . . A wide-mouthed jar with a screw top used for home canning or preserving.

migrant worker . . . . . . A farm laborer who moves from one farm to another to find work.

moldboard plow . . . . . . A type of plow used during the homestead period. It had a curved iron plate that lifted and turned the soil.

monoculture farming . The cultivation of only one crop.

mortgage . . . . Transferring ownership of property to a creditor as a guarantee for a loan.

nomadic . . . . Wandering from place to place.

Okie . . . . Slang term for migrants fleeing from the Dust Bowl or surrounding states due to drought or farm foreclosure.

one-way disk plow . . . . A plow equipped with several sharp, steel disks on an axle. It is pulled behind a tractor.

organism . . . . A living thing.

panhandle . . . . A narrow strip of land attached to a larger territory, such as the panhandle of Oklahoma or Texas.

perennial . . . . [puh-**REN**-ee-ul] A plant that grows year-round.

Phoenicians . . . . [fuh-**NEE**-shuns] Inhabitants of ancient Phoenicia, now known as Lebanon.

relief . . . . Financial assistance from the government.

relic . . . . An object left behind from an earlier time.

respiratory . . . . Having to do with the lungs.

running board . . . . A footboard on the side of an automobile.

sand blow . . . . Sandstorm. A windstorm that raises large clouds of sand.

SCS . . . . Soil Conservation Service, an agency of the U.S. government.

semi-arid . . . . Having light rainfall, usually less than 10 inches (25 centimeters) annually.

sharecropper . . . . A tenant farmer who pays rent with a share of the harvest.

sheaves . . . . Bundles of bound wheat.

shelter belt . . . . A barrier of trees or shrubs that protects crops from strong winds, thereby decreasing erosion.

sod . . . . The upper layer of soil containing the roots and topgrowth of grasses.

species . . . . A scientific classification for a group of living things that can interbreed.

staple . . . . A product regularly used or needed by many people.

subsidize . . . . To aid with public or government money.

tenant farmer . . . . A rent-paying farmer who works land owned by another.

terracing . . . . Land plowed in level steps along a slope to prevent erosion.

threshing . . . . Mechanically separating the seed of a harvested plant from its husk and straw.

till . . . . To plow.

washboard . . . . A board with ridges for scrubbing laundry.

WPA . . . . Works Progress Administration, an agency of the U.S. government.

Further Reading

THE DUST BOWL

Ganzel, Bill. *Dust Bowl Descent*. Lincoln, Nebraska: University of Nebraska Press, 1984.

Howarth, William. "The Okies: Beyond the Dust Bowl." *National Geographic*, September 1984.

Low, Ann Marie. *Dust Bowl Diary*. Lincoln, Nebraska: University of Nebraska, 1984.

Steinbeck, John. *The Grapes of Wrath*. New York: Viking, 1939.

Worster, Donald. *Dust Bowl: The Southern Plains in the 1930s*. New York: Oxford University Press, 1979.

THE GREAT PLAINS

Dick, Everett. *The Sod-House Frontier: 1854-1890*. Lincoln, Nebraska: Johnsen, 1954.

Mayhall, Mildred P. *The Kiowas*. Norman, Oklahoma: University of Oklahoma Press, 1962.

Sandoz, Mari. *The Buffalo Hunters*. New York: Hastings, 1954.

Sandoz, Mari. *The Cattlemen*. New York: Hastings, 1958.

Time-Life. *Grasslands and Tundra*. Alexandria, Virginia: Time-Life, 1985.

THE GREAT DEPRESSION

McElvaine, Robert S. *The Great Depression*. New York: Times Books, 1984.

Other Works Consulted

Aucoin, James. "The Irrigation Revolution and its Environmental Consequences." *Environment*, October 1979.

Bonnifield, Paul. *The Dust Bowl: Men, Dirt, and Depression.* Albuquerque, New Mexico: University of New Mexico Press, 1979.

Braeman, John, Bremner, Robert H. and Brody, David, eds. *The New Deal, Vol. Two.* Columbus, Ohio: Ohio State University, 1975.

Gard, Wayne. *The Great Buffalo Hunt.* New York: Knopf, 1959.

Gray, R.B. *The Agricultural Tractor: 1855-1950.* St. Joseph, Michigan: ASAE, 1956.

Hambridge, Gove, ed. *Climate and Man: Yearbook of Agriculture.* Washington, D C : U.S. Department of Agriculture, 1941.

Hillary, Sir Edmund, ed. *Ecology 2000: The Changing Face of Earth.* New York: Beaufort Books, Inc., 1984.

Hudson, Norman W. "A World View of the Development of Soil Conservation." *Agricultural History*, Spring 1985.

Hurt, R. Douglas. *The Dust Bowl: An Agricultural and Social History.* Chicago: Nelson-Hall, 1981.

Joffe, Joyce et al. *Man, Nature and Ecology.* Garden City, New York: Doubleday, 1974.

Klein, Joe. *Woody Guthrie: A Life.* New York: Knopf, 1980.

Kraenzel, Carl Frederick. *The Great Plains In Transition.* Norman, Oklahoma: University of Oklahoma Press, 1955.

Lydolph, Paul E. "Comparative Drought Strategies: The Soviet Union." *Great Plains Quarterly*, Summer 1986.

Malin, James C. *The Grassland of North America.* Gloucester, Massachusetts: Peter Smith, 1967.

McDean, Harry C. "Dust Bowl Historiography." *Great Plains Quarterly*, Spring 1986.

Meltzer, Milton, ed. *Dorothea Lange: A Photographer's Life.* New York: Farrar, Giroux, Straus, 1978.

Partridge, Michael. *Farm Tools.* Boston: New York Graphic Society, 1973.

Stanley, Jerry. "Children of the Grapes of Wrath." *American West*, January 1986.

Stein, Walter J. *California and the Dust Bowl Migration.* Westport, Connecticut: Greenwood, 1973.

Stryker, Roy E. and Wood, Nancy. *In This Proud Land.* Greenwich, New York: New York Graphic Society, 1973.

Index

The Author, John Farris, is a freelance writer. A graduate of San Diego State University, he lives with his family in Encinitas, California.

Illustrations designed by Maurie Manning capture the drama of the events described in this book.

Manning majored in illustration at Massachusetts College of Art in Boston and has been a professional children's illustrator for more than six years. Her work appears regularly in such magazines as *Children's Digest, Humpty Dumpty,* and *Highlights for Children.*

Manning was assisted by a team of three artists: Michael Spackman, Robert Caldwell, and Randol Eagles. A professional painter for more than nineteen years, Michael Spackman received his training at the High Museum Academy of Art in Atlanta. Robert Caldwell, a graduate of Syracuse University with a degree in fine arts, has been a fine arts professional for eight years. Randol Eagles is a specialist in figurative illustration, and has been a professional illustrator for three years.

Photography Credits

Photos on pages 29 and 35 courtesy of
Kansas State Historical Society
120 West Tenth
Topeka, Kansas 66612

Photo on page 33 from The Depression
Years as Photographed by Arthur Rothstein.
Dover Publications, Inc.
180 Varich Street
New York, New York 10014

Following photos courtesy of
Library of Congress
Photoduplication Service
Washington, DC 20540

page 24 Russell Lee, photographer
page 30 Arthur Rothstein, photographer
page 32 Arthur Rothstein, photographer
page 37 Russell Lee, photographer
page 39 Dorothea Lange, photographer
page 44 Dorothea Lange, photographer